BUMBLEBEE BOOKS
HEART BROKEN MUSINGS

Raunak Agarwal is a storyteller and poet based in Kolkata, India. His first book, *Heart Broken Musings,* a first-of-its-kind Poetry / Rant motivational book was released in 2018 and was an instant bestseller. This is a new edition of the book.

One of the most popular bloggers on Instagram with over 50,000 followers, Raunak considers himself as a jack of all trades, who is slowly, but steadily working towards becoming the master of all of them. He is an avid dreamer and he often turns his bizarre dreams into funny, yet thoughtful short stories. When he's not writing, or dreaming, or making his readers swoon over his poetry, he runs a tax-consultancy firm along with his father.

To stay in touch with him, you can follow him on Instagram: @rk_writes95 or visit his website: https: / / raunakagarwal.com

# HEART BROKEN MUSINGS

RAUNAK AGARWAL

Published by Bumblebee Publishing
An imprint of Shree Balaji International
59, N S Road, 3rd Floor, Room No. 15B,
Kolkata, West Bengal – 700 001
Email: editorialbumblebee@gmail.com

Heart Broken Musings: Rants | Poems | Quotes


ISBN Print Book - 978-81-944818-1-2

*To my late grandfather, Sri Sohan Lal Agarwal.*

*For every teenager, who is in love. For every hooman, who is struggling at life. For the demotivated you, who shall rise again.*

# -Author's Note-

**Once upon a time in Unicorn land, all the unicorns were having a discussion.**

'Why are hoomans so depressed?' one of them pleads.

'Because they are stupid!' the other unicorns exclaimed.

'But we must do something, shouldn't we?' another one asked.

**And after an hour-long debate, the verdict was finally out.**

I, Raunak, your author was brought back from his death-bed to shower us hoomans with motivation and to provide a sarcastic viewpoint to tackle love, life, and everything in between. Because let's face it! We hoomans are obviously stupid and trust me unicorns are never wrong. Did you know? The horn of the unicorn symbolizes ultimate truth and it has the power to pierce the chest of anyone who tries to lie. Damn!

'Uuuuuuuunicornnnnnnnnnnnn,' I yawned, waking up, after being thrown back to our crap-shit called Earth.

'So fellow hoomans, let's begin.'

-O0o-

*"The one good thing about 'death' is that, you can no longer 'disappoint' anyone!"*

*©Raunak Agarwal*

# -000-Death.

Doesn't it make so much sense? Our life can basically be broken into three parts; **Birth-Disappointment-Death**. As long as you are alive, there's nothing you can do to satisfy the people around you. You'll do a thousand good deeds and still, they'll find a way to demean you. It's only when you die and are no longer around, that people realize what your value was, how much you did for them and that you weren't the dill-hole they thought you to be. But ah! It's too late by then.

Wonder, why start with death? Well that's what we fear the most, right? So, why not talk about it, be done with it and start anew. Moreover, it makes so much sense, right? Remember I just came back from my death-bed. So, hello fresh reincarnated souls! Let's take a deep breath and not disappoint anyone for a change.

-O0o-

*"In a world aspiring to be the one,
why do people fear to defy the horoscope
made for everyone!"*

*©Raunak Agarwal*

# -001-You, Yes You.

Now that you survived death and got *reincarnated,* what do you wanna do now? Of course, claim that you're the One! How convenient. And then you wake up in the morning to your daily newspaper and what do you do first? Check your horoscope. Silly you, eh? C'mon! Grow up already. First of all, horoscopes are a bag full of shit! To quote Sheldon Cooper, 'It tells us that you participate in the mass cultural delusion that the sun's apparent position relative to arbitrarily defined constellations at the time of your birth somehow affects your personality' Woah! Someone hit your soft spot.

Anyway, even if you do believe, aren't they made for everyone in general? And if everyone's following the same crap how do you expect that you'll become the crap lord? Stop believing in these myths and do something unique. Be you! Because let me tell you, a horoscope is nothing but a deceive. Ask yourself this, if I tell you that today will be the worst day of your life, would you be able to enjoy that day then? no right? Because your mind is already polluted with the fear that I implanted. See? Thoughts Much!

-O0o-

**Life 101.**

*Look at life through the rains,*
*a drop less; panic, a drop more; pain.*

*Look at life through the rush,*
*every man's for himself, none to trust.*

*Now look at life through the art,*
*Deceivingly it adores, the dull and dark.*

*But when things go all wrong,*
*and nothing feels like real anymore,*
*turn a blind eye and finally,*

*Look at life through your shades,*
*let the filters cleanse this world!*

*©Raunak Agarwal*

# -002-Life 101.

So, you decided to take on life? You've probably kept your past aside by now. Wow, man! I never could. But I'll still give you some literature crap called advice. Follow it and whoosh, you'll succeed! So, who's your life guru? Don't look around. Duh! It's me doofus. So, now that's been decided, *I, Raunak, the reincarnated hooman officially announces himself as the life guru of every single doofus on this planet!* Unicorns (Read: Amen)! Here's a big hi-five from your life guru.

-O0o-

*“Build your empire around those who wish to see you fail.”*

*©Raunak Agarwal*

# -003-Who's The Boss?

Some people trod into your life only for their own convenience, don't they? They make you feel that you mean a whole lot to them. And just when everything falls into place and things seem virtuous, they ditch you! Why? Because they have accomplished their needs. And then, they make excuses, they lie, they assure you into pitiful illusions. That's the bitter truth, but we hoomans don't get that! These are the people to stay away from because they have only one purpose in life! They wish to see you fail. And what's the sweet revenge you can get?

Build your empire around them, folks. Make them cringe their mere existence. Let their mornings be filled with nothing but jealousy. Let that sweet chirps of the birds sing your success tales. Make them sleep with nothing but disappointment. **Build your empire around them and you'll have the last laugh when you rise and those dipshits fail.**

-O0o-

*"The 'Magna cum laude'*
*now struggles to survive.*
*Because getting a 97%*
*can't guarantee you a seat,*
*in the game of life!"*

*©Raunak Agarwal*

# -004-Life: 'Ha Ha'

Remember, how you wanted to become the Number one? Woah! You're the 'Magna cum laude' (the honor given to the topper in many universities). You nailed it! Yay. Or did you? The game of life sucks. Your scores, they used to have immense value during your dad's era but now it's you that sells! The world around you is so dynamic that you need to be an overall package to succeed in the corporate world.

If you thought that your class twelve exams were the most important thing and life after that is all fun and games? Well, welcome to the real world! And in here, all of this matters shit. What can you do anyway? Life is unfair. Get it. And if you think you can make it fair rather than learning to deal with the hypocrisy? You, my friend never was the one! Period.

-O0o-

*“Darling, are you happy with yourself? Trying to find peace in the harsh reality of this glorious mess that you call your life! ”*

*©Raunak Agarwal*

# -005-Darling?

Okay, formatting my work wasn't an easy job, duh. It took hours and hours of editing to get the work perfect and flawless. So, it would mean a great deal to me if you shared the existence of this book with others and made all that effort of mine worthwhile (cries heavily with glee).

Anyway, why am I even complaining when it's about you darling! So, tell me, are you happy? Don't shy away. I know that fuckboy ruined you, your goals are so on track, your cousin; 'Doofus' shifted to America, your best friend got engaged, your dad wants to marry you because he thinks you're a waste. Ah! And yet you enjoy this mess… because the next best thing, well? This is the best you'll ever get. Life is harsh darling and people are stupid. There's so much going around your life and yet you're just a blob. A big blob going nowhere! We hoomans have become addicted to compromise. So much so that we find a certain peace in it. No one likes to be a part of the struggle but everyone wishes to succeed. When will we learn? When will we not compromise with our goals because we faced a few hurdles but keep going along? Maybe never? Well, you know what's glorious, messy and oh I wish it was real? A Unicorn! Someone buy me no? Please? Pretty please? I am still crying please?

-O0o-

*"Forgetting the past is never easy, neither is creating a future. And only you decide where your priorities lie. Choose wisely!"*

*©Raunak Agarwal*

# -006-Ultimate Choice.

Okay, you made a lot of mistakes, you took all the wrong decisions, that super-cool college of yours didn't help you much. What can you do boy? Cry about it? Duh! I know moving-on is not easy but you need to stay positive and think about the amazing times that lie ahead! Get so busy working on your tomorrow that when tomorrow arrives, you'll sip your favorite margarita and chill with it. But you need to act *now*.

Trust me, every day that you waste thinking about your past is only going to pile on to your long list of problems and you don't want that, do you? Here's wishing you a success filled future. I know you'll achieve great heights. All is well.

-O0o-

*❝Thinking about my future and having visions of how successful I'll soon become is, my happy place!❞*

*©Raunak Agarwal*

# -007-Happy Place.

Ah, future again! I so dreamt about being famous recently. And damn, it was sweet! I mean, think about it man. You wake up to a dream of thousands cheering **Raunak Raunak** Omjinkees... Sweeeeeeeet shit! Isn't that an amazing Happy Place? What's yours? Also, the next chapter will be the last chapter of life! Enough with it already. Unless I sneaked in more in the future, maybe? Until then, let's kick life right where it starts shitting lemonades.

Lemonades really? Nah, I need more and more people to read my book. You lovely readers can have the lemonades in return and oh it's *sooooooooo* effing hot in India. Someone, please send me snow right now. Godspeed!

-O0o-

*" An honest man's struggle is a dishonest one's bag of gold! "*

*©Raunak Agarwal*

# -008-The Struggle Is Real.

Remember, last time you got a 95% and were head over heels about it? Well, you know what? I am rich! So even I managed a 95. Yay! In terms of gold though (Read: I bribed officials to get into the top-most college). See that's the harsh reality. Money solves all problems, like literally huh! Damn you, wealth! And this badly hurts the people who actually work hard to earn a day's bread because they don't get the satisfaction they deserve. The rich fellas take it all and the rich keep getting richer and the poor still remain poor.

Then there's this third category called the middle-class **Because too proud to be called poor and no money to be called rich**. These people? Well, they go nowhere. I feel these are the most unfortunate because they keep striving for more money, are never happy, everyone screws them and well they basically have no life! Retards, I tell you.

-OOo-

*“ A broken heart sings the best lullabies! ”*

*©Raunak Agarwal*

# -009-Lalalala.

Gosh! Love is so depressing. It's like; yes, this one. I like his smile, so this crap-head's going to ruin the rest of my life! Yay! People, I tell you? Our Indian culture is so different from the western world, you know? You people have so much freedom when it comes to choosing a soulmate. In fact, you even audition each other in bed before falling in love (pun intended)! Do you know what we do?

Our parents first marry us to an unknown doofus out of nowhere and then the entire community forces us to fall in love! Woah! No wonder we Indians are good singers. Also, a heart in love whistles! Does anyone feel like whistling with me? I'll take you on a unicorn ride! *Lalalalala...*

-O0o-

*" And five years from now,*
*I'll still fall in love with you.*
*As we dance to the 'charade',*
*of your favorite tunes,*
*until the point I wake-up! "*

*©Raunak Agarwal*

# -010-Charade.

Charade <Noun> - An act or event that is clearly false! You had an 'Aww' moment reading it no? Don't lie, I know you did. Think about the moment you tell this to your lover! And she is like; 'Ya whatever.' Well, this is reality! Just as how the guy here still thinks of his love but only in dreams, true love exists only in dreams. In fact, we now love only so we can cheat!

But yes, exceptions are always there! There still are couples who love each other no matter what. You know, I think those people are aliens! Imagine; they fight, one says – 'I need a break.' And the other one goes like – 'Oh please! What are you, *Hooman?*'

-O0o-

***What do girls actually seek in a relationship?***

*The one thing I was sure,*
*no matter how much we fight,*
*ours was a love, pledged for life.*

*And if things went wrong,*
*out of control, our bond shall*
*be the healer of my stubborn soul.*

*We'd go back to the start,*
*to one of those times, when I*
*wasn't yours and you weren't mine.*

*I shall try all those tricks,*
*that once made you woo, and*
*we'll start our journey afresh, anew.*

*And if need be my love,*
*I would do it all again, cause*
*somethings in the world never change.*

# -011-Starting Over.

Since I was talking about true love last time, I thought why not take It a step deeper... So much so that it becomes Surreal! That's the irony of love you know, too much of it becomes cliché. Seriously though, Aren't these goals? I would give anything to find someone who's ready to start over. Trust me, I would! **You might have a thousand flaws, you might be a pain in the ass, but you are my pain in the ass! And I love you! And that's a reason enough for me!**

-O0o-

*"He loved her a lot,*
*she liked him a lot,*
*by the time love and like*
*became synonyms,*
*she was married and*
*he wasn't alive."*

©Raunak Agarwal

# -012-Who's The Bitch?

Sometimes, the person you love the most also loves you a lot and yet there isn't a happy ending? You know why? Because feelings, well they play games, and we are never sure about how we truly feel about someone unless we lose them. Another major fact being time. Sometimes everything is right but timing screws up. And on some other days, we keep looking for a better person and the best one slips away.

So, *who's the bitch?* Is it feelings? Is it time? Or is it you who is never satisfied with what you have in life? Ah, well! Yet, there's this one thing in the world for which love, feelings and timing are always synonymous! Any guess? **Takes a bow while I announce his name** - A Quattro-Formaggi Cheese Burst Pizza!

-O0o-

*❝Anyone who has the
ability to see beauty
doesn't stop at the lights,
but also goes beneath it! ❞*

*©Raunak Agarwal*

# -013-Beauty.

All the talk about love and none about the keyword that love revolves around? Silly me, eh! What is beauty to you anyway? Is it only something that burns your selfish desires? Or is it more than that? Is the idea of falling for souls mere hypocrisy to you? No-one likes the dark man! All the gold that glitters! Once you lose your shine, nobody will stick with you, they'll leave!

I recently saw this video where this girl was like, 'I can't marry him, our selfies don't come good.' Really woman? Your selfies aren't beautiful? Damn! Look beyond what shines folks. Because trust me, *the real beauty lies within.*

-O0o-

*"They both were in love;*
*had their own ways!*
*One kissed her in the dark,*
*the other protected her*
*when she was frail.*
*The first won her body,*
*the latter won her soul!"*

*©Raunak Agarwal*

# -014-Body Or Soul?

I bet you'll read this one over and over again and still not get enough of it! A love triangle like no other. So, who was the hero here? Who really won? That's the difference between love and lust! Lust seeks your body. They care if you are hot, if you applied that mascara right, if you are going to get them laid today. That is not love... damn! *True love goes for souls!* They care if you are happy, they care about the reason that mascara is not on point, they wanna take you for long walks, they remember the little things you do and say.

Get it? Basically, one cares for their own happiness and the other cares for yours! Who will you seek darling? Choice, choice?

-O0o-

*" Our smiles were the best 'deceivers', like a month-old wine! I never questioned her intentions and she never doubted mine. "*

*©Raunak Agarwal*

# -015-Month Old Wine.

Okay! What's better? Being frank about the fact that it's not working anymore or silently bearing the pain because you don't want the other person to be hurt? Or, what about a relationship like this one where both are happily 'Not in love'! People sure are innovating. Damn! For all those who don't know, wine is a symbol of rich taste but only if it's years old. So, you get it? A month-old wine is such a smart deceive! Similarly, our smiles hide away so much of our emotions.

Picture this! I am smiling at you. You start blushing. We come close for that tight hug. And bam! I stab you with a smile (read knife)! Trust me if you don't spread the word about this book, I will find you and smile at you so hard you'd probably stab yourself.

-O0o-

*“Owing to the shackles*
*of their families,*
*they both eloped!*
*His; the first of last,*
*hers; the first of many!”*

*©Raunak Agarwal*

# -016-Eloped.

This one can be interpreted in two ways. Sometimes you know, everything works out just as fine, all the stars are in place, you feel so elated and bam! Life throws yet another shackle at you! 'Family'. Tsk tsk. The poor couple hence had no other choice but to elope! But things don't end there, at least not for the girl. Running away is just the first step, the girl needs to handle the people around her, thc society, the guy and if they have kids! She's basically screwed. **Author salutes to all the women**.

On the contrary, think of it in this way. The guy loved her truly and was ready to elope, she was her one true love. But for the girl? Well, she'd have her fun. He's just one of the many lovers she'll elope with. That bitch! **The army sees the author signaling and they shoot all women at the salute!**

-O0o-

*"Distressed by cultural taboos,*
*the Sarpanch's daughter*
*played the joker card!*
*Proudly yet 'unfortunately',*
*now her desk plate reads,*
*'Mr.' Aarti Chauhan, IAS officer. "*

*©Raunak Agarwal*

# -017-Sex Change Anyone?

Well! Women and their struggles. I do feel you guys. Why is it never easy for you all? Look what she did. When the society weighed her down, she switched to the acceptable gender. She is a respected officer now, she'll fight the system from the inside, she'll get equal rights for women, too bad she'll be the last of it. Cause 'Mr. Aarti' cannot have kids now, tsk! But, on the bright side? She can literally screw all those who look down upon her **Cough-Prosthetic-Dick-Cough**.

I don't understand hoomans. Why do they consider women inferior? When will they get an equal opportunity? You know what? Never! Not until Trump keeps grabbing women by the pussy and Priyanka is shamed for sitting bare legs with Mr. Modi.

P.S. - **Sarpanch is the Government head assigned to a village in India**IAS officer is the topmost Government job in India**Trump is the US President**Trump grabs women by their pussy**Priyanka is a Bollywood actress (Feat Quantico, Baywatch)**Narendra Modi is the Indian Prime Minister**He is considered the next Hitler in the business world**

-O0o-

***Will this society ever accept me?***

*My birth wasn't a miracle,*
*for no-one really smiled.*
*Through endless bias and taunts,*
*I taught myself to fly.*
*I had such flourishing Desires,*
*but was always looked down.*
*To prove this world my worth,*
*I tried but was frowned.*
*Teresa, Oprah, Malala,*
*could have been my inspirations.*
*But Silence, Compromise, Torture,*
*were my eventual destinations.*
*So yes, I am a woman,*
*and yes, I have a question!*
*Will this society ever accept me?*

*©Raunak Agarwal*

# -018-Teresa, Oprah, Malala.

This one, I wrote for Women's Day. So Happy Women's Day all of you! Now, I could try and explain my poetry but really? Do I need to? My words speak so much already.

Just remember, if you're a woman! Pat on your back now. You guys are amazing. And I don't know if the society can, but when this book becomes super-famous and I become President of Unicorn land, I'll accept you all and we'll ride unicorns together!

-O0o-

*Dear BFF,*

*We could be a couple in a thousand alternative universes but never be as happy as we are as friends in this one!*

*Sincerely,*
*Raunak Agarwal**

**The guy who loves you too much to survive a breakup!*

# -019-Open Letter (BFF)

Hey best friend, you know what? I love you. I love you, way too much. And you know what this means? If I were to ever lose you, I probably won't survive. People these days make a lot of promises but in the end, they just leave and that happens to me a lot! Can you promise me a forever even if it's as friends? Can you not leave? Lovers are so lame! They have a fight and the first thing that comes to their mind is a break-up.

But when two friends fight, it only makes their bond stronger. Friendship is a unique thing, it's way too pure than love. And if you have someone with whom you can share your world without the fear of them judging you, you are goddamn lucky.

-O0o-

*Dear Parents,*

*It's my life, let me get screwed, let me lose, that's how I'll learn and grow, but please don't try and make me someone you guys couldn't become. After-all, we're the same genes, isn't it?*

*Sincerely,*
*Raunak Agarwal*

# -020-Open Letter (Parents)

There's this thing about parents, they want their children to fulfill their so-called dream. But, oh! Don't you get it father? You couldn't do it. How can I? Moreover, at least you wanted to do it, you probably worked for it, I don't even want to, duh! This should be an eye-opener for parents. We are the same fucking Genes! Don't you pressure me into a life filled only with regret?

I respect your wishes but I know my caliber and I'll be the best in what I can do. Can I please focus on that? Can you not pressure me into shit? I love you dad, I...

-O0o-

**Nearing his death, the old man finally read the last letter his dead wife had written**

*Dear love,*

*Promise me, when you arrive in heaven, you shall find me and we'll knot again. Only this time our vows shall read, 'Till life do us apart'*

*Forever yours,*

**And love had a whole new meaning**

*©Raunak Agarwal*

# -021-Open Letter (Love)

You've heard 'Till death do us apart' but remember, it's me? And it's my book! Everything has a different viewpoint. Isn't this letter goals? A love beyond life. A love that doesn't end with death. A love beyond horizons. If I read this letter, I would have felt like dying right now. If only I could find someone worthy of true love, though. Remember, we live in a stupid world. And guess who else is stupid? Your ex! Who had once promised you a forever. True love has so become like a unicorn these days. It's become a myth.

Just in these recent months! I have seen at-least four divorces and that too for stupid reasons. Gosh, it really hurts. **Pyaar toh hamare purvaj karte the; zindagi ke sath bhi, zindagi ke baad bhi!** (Love truly existed during the time of our ancestors, from the day of getting married to even beyond death)

-O0o-

*“There’s this one big flaw in the concept of love! People always claim to either fall or rise in love but no-one ever claims of staying in it! ”*

*©Raunak Agarwal*

# -022-Stay in Love?

Ah, this is a big one. The secret is out guys! Your life guru has revealed why love fails so much. Hey girl! I fell in love with you. Girl, I am falling for you. Girl, you made my jaws drop (read fall). **kitta giroge bhai? Ab toh teri aukaat bi puch rahi hogi... Mere Se bi niche gir gaye?** Love never promises a steady journey. If you survive, you'd rise, else you'd fall. But oh why? Why can't we promise of staying in love? Why not say something like... Woman, I love you and we'll stay in love, together; forever!

Gosh! If love had an advertisement, it would probably be like *Anything that falls or rises is subject to market risks! Stalk everything about the person carefully before loving.*

-O0o-

*“The moon only looks this beautiful,
because the sun lends its rays to it!
Go be the sun in someone’s life and
shine when they see the moon in you!”*

*©Raunak Agarwal*

# -023-My Moon.

It's time to focus on you darling. I know you want a fairy tale life. I know the kind of dreams you have. But the Moon is only a mere blob of (something). It has no value unless the Sun is there, shining its rays on it. All I am saying is, beauty starts with you but it only stays with how you treat others. You got to inspire people, influence them, make them special. And damn! They'll see the moon in you. That's when you'll really shine! You'll blush like there's no tomorrow and that shall be the real fairy tale you always wished for.

Who's the moon of your life? Who has always been there whenever you felt sad, whenever you were blue? Who's been through your thick and thin always encouraging you to stay shining? Call them and bring a shine on their faces!

-O0o-

***Deep Blue Sky!***

*"Hey soulmate,*
*let's aim so high.*
*Prospering together,*
*to the clouds we fly.*
*Promise me your love,*
*till the point you die.*
*For I'll never get tired,*
*of the deep blue sky! "*

*©Raunak Agarwal*

# -024-Deep Blue Sky.

Could I have summed-up love better than that? What's the point of loving if you both don't succeed together. A relationship that seeks to bring out the best in both of you. A promise to keep loving till eternity. Where you don't ever get tired of your partner. That's the love I want! Canvassing the deep skies, fluttering our wings of success.

-O0o-

*❝ 'Tween fading affection,*
*fake love, and growing insecurities,*
*we reminded each-other,*
*our promise to never fall apart,*
*so, we switched to cheating! ❞*

*©Raunak Agarwal*

# -025-Cheating.

Screw the above quote! I know it's wow. But today your life guru will rant about himself. Recently a friend of mine broke up with his girlfriend almost a month after they got physical. Ask me why? Because he didn't like her behavior and how she treated the people around him. I was naturally disturbed and feeling how hurt she must be, asked him to give her another chance! And he was like... 'No man! There's no attachment right now. So, it's good to end now. What if I start developing feelings? I won't be able to leave her later! So, it's best to end now.'

Dafuq dude! No feelings, no attachment? You guys hooked up man. All without any kind of affection? The fuck is wrong with this world! I see people like these and feel like... Am I too nice to be hooman? I am someone who doesn't give a shit about others. I'll ignore you like hell... But once I get to know you... You'll consider me as the best thing that ever happened to you. I'll be forever ready to help you out. I don't get attached easily but once I do, it gets so hard when people simply screw you and leave. And here was this friend who never got attached at all! Gosh, it must be sweet to keep hopping from one person to the other? Right? You know what? Relationships these days be like, **Number exchange. Late night chats. Goof around. Get bored. Repeat** Is love even real anymore? Thoughts?

-O0o-

*"Do you know that one quality of hoomans that dooms us all?*

*- Perspective "*

*©Raunak Agarwal*

# -026-I Am Me.

We hoomans live in a world of fear. All of us have immense talent but that stupid fear of how people will react to our work is a big barrier. The world is such you know... It's almost impossible for us to survive if we start pursuing our dreams. It's either the world's way or it's no way… like I am a writer! But that's not going to earn me my bread and butter. I got to do something to earn a living, right? But why? Why is it so tough? Duh. Your family, your relatives. Even your neighbors. Everyone has an opinion if you do something out of blues. They all expect you to be the herd and keep chewing that lame-ass grass.

Dafuq people? *I am Me!* I'll do whatever I feel like. I'll not grow carrots on my farm. I'll breed Unicorns. Do you have a problem? You can go kiss your sorry *Perspective's ass!*

-O0o-

*"Ever looked at something so messed up and yet so beautiful?*
*- Yes, a dreamer's eyes!"*

*©Raunak Agarwal*

# -027-Messed Up.

Tihs is yuor lfie gruu Ranuak rpetornig for dtuy. Ah! You still managed to read it no? That's how awesome you are. The world around us is a big blob of mess. And the only way you can survive? You got to dream! Dream big. People who have a vision, a purpose are the ones who are always ahead of the race. Look into their eyes, and you'll see a beauty like no other. The beauty of success. Everyone dreams at night, right? But not all of you remember it? You know why? Because your mind has already given up on you. You, lazy moron! **jk, it's a normal thing.**

But people who are successful, they don't just see dreams. They act upon it. Look into their eyes and you'll see how much they are struggling, how messed up they are, how much they get their ass kicked on a daily basis.

And damn! When you do, make sure you don't fall in love with them because these people are already committed! Committed to success, committed to fame; wealth; honor. Ah! Such nerds, right? **pun intended**

Then there are people who'll sleep from 9 pm to 9 am and then blame everything on karma *Did I ever tell you karma is a bitch?* well, messed up is always beautiful! Because who ever gave a damn to the sorted ones? *_*

-O0o-

*"And in a perfect world with perfect genes;*
*we'd still fall for the wrong person!"*

*©Raunak Agarwal*

# -028-Genes.

To err is to hooman. To motivate is to Raunak Agarwal. Imagine a world where everything is perfect, you are at the epitome of success and this fuck boy walks-up to you in torn jeans, shabby looks but a shit load of money. What do you do? Fall in love with him? No doofuses... You guys are my students, you don't fall in love, you stay in love xD **Author pats his back** But wait! Where did the fuck boy come from? Aren't we in a perfect world?

I'll tell you! What are we? Hoomans. What do we do? Find faults. I gave you a perfect world, and you madam, discovered a fuck boy. Bravo! **Newton hits himself with an apple** that's the thing. We always end up finding faults in people. To us no-one is perfect. No-one is the best. We hoomans are never satisfied with what we have. And in our attempt to find the best doofus, we reject so many good ones, that we got to settle for a fuck boy.

Ah, well! Neither is the world going to be perfect ever nor did science perfect genes yet so it's better I shut-up and you go find faults in others. Cheers.

-O0o-

*Happy Father's Day!*

*I was a piece of 'Overdramatic Melodrama',*
*and you were the one, who taught me life.*
*Hiding your struggles; to make me glee,*
*to wiping my tears, whenever I'd cry.*
*In a world of google, of books, of friends,*
*you were my teacher, my know-it-all.*
*And whenever at our work, I'd screw,*
*you would be my shield, to take the fall.*
*In a system that's corrupt, of lies and shit,*
*your one rule, to speak the truth prevailed,*
*a naive hooman, I was, dumb, stubborn.*
*You lessoned me wits, whenever I failed.*
*From 'Johny Johny, yes papa', to,*
*'Johnnie Walker, yes papa',*
*Happy Father's Day!*

*©Raunak Agarwal*

# -029-Hey Dad.

On 17th June, we celebrated Father's Day in India! And the entire social media was bonkers over posting pictures with their dads. Really folks? Is one day enough for the very person who bought you that smartphone for posting? But it's okay, Indian dads are savages, they are hard nut-shells who really don't respond to emotions. You walk up to your dad and tell him, *'Dad I turned 18 today' and he'll be like, 'when I was your age, I was 19'.*

Anyway, when it comes to my dad! We really don't see eye to eye, ego clashes you know? But yesterday, I might have not wished him, but I spent the entire day with him and I guess that's sweet enough of me? **Cloud nine feels**

-O0o-

*Suicide note - ✓*
*Razor blades - ✓*
*Courage..........?*

**And the reason she failed in life 'ironically' became the reason of her survival.**

# -030-1 Reason Why Not.

Much irony eh? We hoomans fear a lot. You give us something to do and the first emotion that fills our spine is that of fear. But we are greedy. We are forever ready to jump the ship we have no intention to pilot. Look around you... You'll find so many people trying to achieve a thousand things at the same time and as a result, failing miserably. And hush! Failure brings us so down in this cruel society that not everyone can cope up with its adversaries. That's where courage comes in. When people fail and find no purpose to live, these wackos turn to suicide as an option. But, even that's not easy, is it? Killing yourself by slitting those wrists is not an easy job. You need a lot of *jigra* (courage) for that.

If you ask me? I'll probably suck at killing myself! I'll start slitting wrists, and at the very first drop of blood, whoosh! I'll faint. Btw does that really solve a problem? Suicide is overrated. You don't kill yourself by committing suicide. You murder the people who cared for you; your parents who raised you, your friends who were your drop of happiness, and many such others. Tsk.

So, fellas! Pat your back! Fluff your chest! Look in the mirror! And yell 'I can survive'. Yell for your life! Please don't murder your loved ones. Please don't kill yourself.

-O0o-

*"There are all the colors in the world
and then there's ¥0U!"*

*©Raunak Agarwal*

# -031-Colors.

People! They have so many colors I tell you. You'd figure out one and whoosh they'll switch to another. There's no understanding someone. And yet amongst all the chameleons out there, I found you. The one unique person! You were different. Because you gave a shit about you and you yourself. To you, the world mattered nothing at all. Yes, I am talking about you. But who are we kidding? Close your eyes and answer me! Are you really the bad-ass you keep proving? Aren't you that soft little fluff of wool you'd want everyone to cuddle to? Aren't you someone who needs all the attention in this world? You'd probably be like? Damn! How does he know so much?

Remember I have been examining you all for the last thirty-one chapters. Anyway, stop pretending woman because well, it's only when you'll come out in the open will the unicorns reveal themselves. Don't you wanna see unicorns? Your true colors are the one, people will fall in love with. *Those crimson shades of blue mixed with mellow pink will make people swoon and damn! When you'll flip those long gorgeous hairs. I tell you. Girl! I so tell you.*

PS: Hey, you special person reading this book! This chapter is to each and every one of you who've made this book a success up till now. All of you who read my books are the unique hoomans this world deserves. Here's giving you all a twenty-one-unicorn's salute.

-O0o-

*" Let her escape into the world free,*
*cage her not, lest her wings shalt die,*
*embrace the colors of her glory glee,*
*and when she flutters, you'd be her pride! "*

*©Raunak Agarwal*

# -032-Girl Child.

Society, are you on dope? Why is your motto something like 'Women are our pride! So, we will keep them hidden safely inside our four walls so that no one can see them.' That's not how you embrace pride. It's been a long time that you've kept them locked. But now, no more! She's had enough. She's about to wither away.

So, let her be free now. Let her enjoy this new-found freedom. Let her achieve something tremendously beautiful. And when she does that, each and every ounce of her success will have your and only your name! And that's how you'll embrace her pride. Period.

-O0o-

*“I took a road of pricks and thorns,*
*en-route a solemn boom,*
*at my peak, she graced her fate,*
*and love conceived our doom!”*

*©Raunak Agarwal*

# -033-Doom.

*Umm... Humpty Dumpty fell in love, Humpty Dumpty so got fucked! All the world's money and all the wise men. Couldn't put Humpty together again.* Poor fellow, eh! Was so focused on his work. Probably went through a shit load of troubles and barriers with only one motive in mind... Success! But ah this destiny! Just when everything was going perfect, the wise-ass blonde comes swooping into his life and instead of everything falling in place, our Humpty falls down.

They say behind every successful person is a woman. Yes! A woman who screwed his life so hard that the person had no choice but to be successful and prove it to her face! Our Humpty was unlucky in this matter and the blonde being a cunning leech ran away with all his money. Tsk. These kinds of things happen. There are people who become acquainted with you for the sole purpose of leeching off you. Be wary of them. Make sure you are in the right kind of company and remember, the road to success is a one-person lane, it's always taken alone!

P.S. - I took a guy's perspective but the same is obviously true for women. Please don't kill me for demeaning women. You need motivation in the future, right?

-O0o-

***Is love really worth revenge?***

*A choice so big, she gushed!*
*She feared, yet chose to smile.*
*Of the 'Jealous' and the Crus'he'd,*
*aghast! the Latter, parted by.*
*For love's disheartening, swayed.*
*He reasoned with anger, sighed!*
*Through silence, revenge shall take.*
*With a grin, escaped a 'hi'.*
*Her fears; that storm did calm.*
*For her heart had made its peace.*
*Perjury to one, honesty to none,*
*all that 'juggling' got her pissed!*
*Vengeance earned, yet lessons unheeded,*
*how long do we hide our mistakes?*

*©Raunak Agarwal*

# -034-Revenge?

She is facing a Dilemma involving two people. One who truly loves her and the other who is simply jealous of her closeness with the former. She chooses the jealous! But why? Anyway, the lover decides to leave. But leaving is making things easy! Isn't it? So, he makes a comeback. But how long can one keep juggling the heart and the soul? Knock knock? Karma! Still, is love really worth revenge?

-O0o-

*❝ I thought she was a star,*
*the ones that twinkle.*
*She turned out to be the Sun,*
*and burnt me alive! ❞*

*©Raunak Agarwal*

# -035-My Star Or Sun?

**Unfortunately I kept staring at her; that's where I went wrong!** There's this Indian saying, 'If Lemons never had seeds, It could make people immortal.' and 'if Guavas never had seeds it could kill people' Woah! Right? How many of you have heard about it?

It's the same with people, you expect them to be something but there's this hidden trait inside of them which is not easily revealed. Everyone's unique but not necessarily in a good way! And the problem is that by the time we find out who the other person really is, it's often too late and we hoomans as a process suffer, ah well!

-O0o-

*❝ Somewhere in the chaos of*
*your heart and brain, there's a*
*cell screaming, 'Yes, I can!'*
*Take me there. ❞*

*©Raunak Agarwal*

# -036-Yes, I Can.

**That's the cell that needs all the protein.** We hoomans are sluggish. Until and unless someone slaps that lazy ass of ours, we don't budge an inch. For instance, tell me to go somewhere or do something, I'll simply sleep over it.

People often ask me, 'I read so much of motivation but when it comes to actually apply them, I fail One Big Time!'. To all of those, I know we are lazy. I know we are nothing but a big blob of potato. But there must be one unique moment in each of our lives when we decided to not act as a lazy ass and actually do something, right? And damn! The rewards for not being a doofus for a change must have been really sweet.

That's all the motivation you need. Reading motivation is not going to get you motivated. it's just literature crap you know. You yourself are your biggest motivator and only your past achievements can turn that lazy ass of yours into a worthy one! Period.

-O0o-

*❝ And darling, why do you ask for an escape? When you as a child would cage that firefly because it was beautiful? ❞*

*©Raunak Agarwal*

# -037-Fireflies.

Darling, you told me yesterday that you were done with society. You were done with life! People treat you with disrespect, they demean you. They don't let you do anything your way. Your family, friends, lover, they act as if they own you! I know that's how our **Ultra-Social-Hypo-dramatic-Society** functions, but before you think of doing anything to yourself, think about it?

Don't assume that this society is above you. In fact, it's so afraid of you that it fears that once you get those wings, you'll take the world under your control! It's this fear of the society that's keeping you caged. Darling, trust me, you are and will be the most beautiful thing in this world but being beautiful comes at a price, right?

I know it's going way too far, that too when times have changed, people have changed; the irony has evolved. The beautiful Firefly won't be caged now. It shall soon shine and flicker. But will YOU? Can you promise me to survive only that much longer?

-O0o-

*❝ And if it rained, it wasn't your heart,*
*but the universe that made you*
*fall in love with her! ❞*

*©Raunak Agarwal*

# -038-The Universe.

**Diary - Page 1. It was raining. She offered to share her umbrella**. And it was the beginning of a beautiful love story, blessed by the complicity of the rain.

As Paulo Coelho once said, 'And when you want something, all the universe conspires to help you achieve it.' Rains are magical and at the same time lucky for they have witnessed quite a lot of love stories. Maybe they are the real cupids people keep talking about?

Because when two people meet amidst the beauty of the rains, it's not the bodies but their souls that connect. And, no-one plans to woo someone using rain now? It's a natural thing. It's not what your heart desired. It's what the universe had set in mind.

Maybe he/she is the soul-mate you've been searching all this while? Maybe he/she is the fire to your ice? Maybe he/she is, in fact, the person with whom you not only want to share an umbrella but an entire lifetime? Maybe? Thoughts?

-O0o-

***Hues and Fire.***

*One day, this sky,*
*will flaunt its hues.*
*But promise you, darling! I,*
*wouldn't let you be blue.*
*In this gleam of shine,*
*we will mask our duress.*
*To the heavens divine,*
*our love, shall we confess.*
*And if ever in my life,*
*I dare feel the cold.*
*Yours would be the hand,*
*I'll, forever and always hold.*
*For how long, can we hide desire?*
*One day, this world shall see fire!*

*©Raunak Agarwal*

# -039-Hues and Fire.

Yes, my love... One day this world shall see fire and that will be the best day of our lives. So, guys, what do you think about this poem and how do you interpret it. I am not writing any flashy author notes in this chapter. Don't kill me for that.

-O0o-

*"On a scale of 1 to 10,*
*you'll always be my 10.5!"*

*©Raunak Agarwal*

# -040-My Momo.

**But if you ask me? I'd probably say six. Just the way I call you a Momo when you ask me for a compliment** Everyone has that one special person in their lives who mean the world to them and no matter what that person does or how messed up that person is, they will always be perfect for us. And yet we never show our affection towards them openly. Rather, we tease them, insult them (in a fun way) because that's what bonding really is, right?

I know you're beautiful and yet I'll call you a Momo or maybe a potato for that matter. Because, even you understand that when I call you a Momo; what I actually mean is, 'You're gorgeous and I am lucky that you're a part of my life! You're the forever I always wished for. You're the star that twinkles only to make me shine. You're the smile that brings a curve to my face. And you're the Momo that I'd eat even when I'm sick.'

P.S. Momo is a South-Asian dumpling dish. It's a type of steamed bun with some form of filling.

-O0o-

*"Life is too short to simply talk to people, manipulate them instead!"*

*©Raunak Agarwal*

# -041-Too Short?

You have around seventy to seventy-five years of life to live, right? Of that, the first five years are well meh! And so are the last ten. So, do you really wanna spend sixty goddamn years just talking to people? Late realization.

There's so much to do man! So much to achieve! And the world is such you got to make others tiptoe at your fingers. Only then will you get your desires fulfilled. Manipulation is nuclear of the future and only those who are cunning, wicked, and smart enough to make use of the people around them will survive.

It's your choice anyway, what do you wanna be? A person who spent an entire lifetime simply talking to people or a person who is talked about for centuries? Thoughts much?

-O0o-

***Slum Life!***

*We grew up in a poor slum.*
*No care, no love, no life!*
*Respect and Status; we had none,*
*so I earned myself 'Teacher's pride'.*

*I always wanted a melon farm.*
*All I needed were seeds.*
*It cost's money which I had none,*
*so I knocked-up 'Meloned teens'.*

*I got a work in the city scrapes,*
*A top-secret job indeed.*
*One night in lockup and I realized,*
*they had made me sell 'weed'!*

*With regret, returned home,*
*to my parents, daughter, and wife.*
*Hoping in Eternity I'd rise again.*
*At Night, I dined on 'Cyanide'!*

*Poverty, Intolerance, Struggles*
*were my many proud names.*
*If only our leaders would invest in me,*
*would this verse still be a shame?*

# -042-Slum Lord.

This is a satirical poem on poverty and in no way, is directed towards any community, caste or gender.

-O0o-

*“No, I don’t love you anymore,
I rather envy you for having a taste
of something as beautiful as me
and yet being strong enough
to not fall in love. ”*

*©Raunak Agarwal*

# -043-Envy You?

At times... You have so long been screwed that you simply forget the idea of being loved. To you, love or any other feeling for that matter becomes mere hypocrisy. Life teaches us a lot of things. But in our aim to not screw up again... In our aim to prove this world that we are stronger, we end up ignoring the beauty around us as well.

We get so caught up in correcting the worst that the good doesn't even matter. We end up treating the rare kindness that we get with disrespect; maybe because we are not ready to accept the fact that things can take a positive turn. We forever struggle with the idea of staying strong and not letting our guard down... And well, we fail!

Remember one thing, not everyone's the same, not everyone's here to screw you and not everyone is a heartless blob! So, the next time you shoo away a good thing because the past has always been meh? For a change, think with your stupid heart. Yes! Be stupid. Don't be afraid that you'll be shit upon. Cause trust me! **Being strong is not about staying away from shit, It's about handling shit.**

-O0o-

*"The world could have been my oyster.*
*But I was born a vegetarian!"*

*©Raunak Agarwal*

# -044-My Oyster.

Lazy procrastinators always have an excuse for what they don't do because that's their thing! Who says procrastinators don't do shit? They make excuses and that's not an easy thing to do, right? Everyone's born to rule, that's how God made us. **Except for Trump, Pretend-Feminists and Racists Of course. They are born to be assassinated**

All it takes for you is to get out from that comfy bed and haul ass! Work for your goals and at the same time make sure you enjoy it. Because you can only be satisfied if you are happy. Big deal you're a vegetarian? So, you cannot eat oysters? At least you can pretend to eat one? So what you are not at the epitome of prime? You can pretend to be one? And maybe all that pretending might actually motivate your lazy ass to work hard and make it big for real? But you got to try first! Only then shall you know.

-O0o-

*"You always complain about*
*little things," they said.*
*"You love me so much that even*
*the smallest thing affects you,"*
*they never said!*

*©Raunak Agarwal*

# -045-Little Things.

Relationships these days have become a pain in the ass. All couples go through phases of love. And there comes a time in our crappy relationship when at least one of us starts getting affected by even the smallest thing that the other person does. And well, not everyone takes that in a positive way.

We get annoyed, start feeling tied up, consider the person too clingy, keep nagging for freedom and whatnot. And that's the end of it! The next thing you know? You're blocked! But why? Isn't it like a natural thing? If someone deeply loves you, isn't it goals that the other person gets affected by little things? Wouldn't you want a life partner who cares so much about you?

Nah! You need a meat-loaf, a heartless, emotionless meat-loaf! And then you'll complain that the meat is undercooked? Or, maybe, you'll say you don't eat non-veg. Duh! Why such hypocrisy? Why even buy meat when you're getting pie? when life is already giving you lemons, why do you have to complain about it?

-O0o-

*❝ And now when I lose someone,*
*I might behave like I don't give*
*a damn... But deep down in*
*my heart, *I've become*
*less of a hooman! ❞*

*©Raunak Agarwal*

# -046-Less Hooman?

I have been screwed. I have been screwed a lot of times and well? I am proud of it! Because it's taught me numerous life lessons. And I can never forget these lessons because this is what I am now. This is what defines me. Unfortunately, not everyone is capable of coping with being screwed over and over again.

After a time... People simply go into denial. It gets so worse, that you walk up to a random person... And you'd find him/her smiling, smiling for no reason at all. But, don't let that fool you though, because behind that pointless smile is a withered piece of skeleton that has long lost its soul. The adversaries of life got so deep in its roots that he/she could simply not survive.

Again, the person is not dead, at least not in the literal sense but he/she isn't alive either. What you're looking at is merely a soulless body living just for the sake of it. A body that waits for its inevitable death. A being that's lost any purpose to live. A person who's become less of a hooman.

**I really don't give a damn!*

-O0o-

*"It was the 'silence' after we fought, which made me realize that I'd rather fight with you than love someone else!"*

# -047-Silence.

Do you know what being in love is like? **It's like you're a rocket, the person you love the fuel and the entire world has the remote!** Love has a shit load of hurdles and if you can't handle them, you're screwed! This means that if you are in love you are going to argue quite often, sometimes even on silly issues.

But true love always survives the test of time. If you're truly and deeply in love... Arguing is just a silly thing that you'll do and laugh it off later. Because the silence that follows an argument is something that you two cannot live with.

And obviously, you won't start fooling around with some random doofus *(FRIENDS trivia: Fighting doesn't mean you two are on a BREAK)*. Well, who's got time for that right? Silence does stand as a true Test of love indeed! Cause, if you two aren't together in both the ups and downs of life, why are you two even together? Knock Knock.

-O0o-

*"Two roads diverged in the yellow woods,*
*and I chose the one that led to pizza!"*

*©Raunak Agarwal*

# -048-Robert Frost.

Sorry? Not sorry? Because people disappoint. Only 'Pizza' is eternal. Let's face it, there's no such thing as the road less traveled by. There are people everywhere; stupid, crappy dill-holes poking their nose at every small matter of yours. It's basically a choice between two roads; both filled with people. The only difference being... One is so old that the road has all worn down and there are a lot of cracks on the way... And well the other one has Pizza! It's got all the modern amenities, it's all futuristic and well, it's all you could wish for.

Unfortunately, both the roads lead nowhere. In the end, its nothing but a sweet release of disappointment hidden behind the crap we call our life! That's the truth and you have to face it. Long story short, you can either enjoy the ride or keep slogging for a better one! But, does a better one even exist?

-O0o-

## *Flashback*

*Thou room is set,*
*the curtain down, no sign*
*of 'sun' or 'moon', the knot*
*of air, flick in the wind,*
*light rushes into the room.*
*Stood she in a cradle,*
*her hair glorifying the knees,*
*those eyes so dark, hands*
*pale, lips; a patch of green.*
*Lightning strikes, it starts to*
*rain, she gives an angry grin.*
*I flick my eyes in fear,*
*and she is gone; vanished*
*beyond a flash of memories,*
*Mother, was it you?*

*©Raunak Agarwal*

# -049-Flashback.

I wrote this sonnet when I was in class ten and is amongst the very first ones that I wrote. PS. I have always been bad with heavy words. I thought that cradle is a rocking chair. However, it's a small bed for children. So, for this poem, we'll assume that cradle equals rocking chair.

-O0o-

*❝ Of all the things I should have done*
*and of all the things I did. 'professing'*
*my love to the right person and*
*confessing it to the wrong one*
*is what hurt the most. ❞*

*©Raunak Agarwal*

# -050-Profess Or Confess?

Maybe that's where I went wrong. I Invested so much time in wooing the wrong person that by the time I realized who the right person for me was, it was too late.

Maybe, I started expecting so less from my own life and so much from others that the one good thing that was happening to me after so long became nothing but a bunch of crap. Or maybe the fact that I thought my love for the wrong person was mutual is what went wrong. Or maybe life is a bitch and I am just a doofus?

We as hoomans expect way too much from others without realizing that we are having expectations from a person who doesn't even have expectations for himself! That's it. If the other person is an ass enough to do nothing for himself, how do you expect him/her to do something for you?

Life has become a serious cycle of dilemmas. **Everyone wants someone and that someone also wants someone and it goes on and on and on until all three of them want no-one and that's the end of life.**

-O0o-

*"Everyone wants someone and that someone also wants someone and it goes on and on and on until all three of them want no-one and that's the end of life."*

# Thank You

Loved my book, didn't you? Heart Broken Musings is my first book. I started this book as an attempt to do something unique in the poetry genre. Of the few books I have read over the years, authors often write and then let the world decide how their work should be interpreted. I tried going a step ahead and instead of just writing my quotes, musings, and poetry, I made an attempt to put forward my viewpoint in every chapter. Sometimes people start thinking so deeply that the simplicity of the work gets lost. Each one of my rants speaks about what I had in mind when I came up with that particular piece. How I wanted to portray my feelings. How, when I said that 'The sky is blue,' I did not mean that the sky is a unicorn but that the sky is simply blue.

Please don't forget to review my book on Amazon or Flipkart. Also, do share a word or two about this amongst your friends and closed ones inviting them to be a part of Heart Broken Musings and help this budding writer reach a wider audience. Thank you from the bottom of my heart for reading my emotions. Glad we connected. After all, words are the most intimate form of bonding, isn't it? Much unicorns.

– Raunak Agarwal

BY THE SAME AUTHOR

*The Things We Do for Love*

*Paralyzed in Dreamland*

www.ingramcontent.com/pod-product-compliance
Lightning Source LLC
LaVergne TN
LVHW031426170726
843492LV00009B/2878

* 9 7 8 8 1 9 4 4 8 1 8 1 2 *